THINE THE GLORY

Thine The Glory

by

Wyn Blair Sutphin

Foreword by Dr. Norman Victor Hope
Professor of Church History,
Princeton Theological Seminary

E. P. DUTTON & CO., INC.
New York   1962

Library of Congress Catalog Card Number: 62-9127

to

My Private Angel

FOREWORD

The sermons which make up the present volume do not require any recommendation from me or from anyone else. But, as a former teacher and long-time friend of the author, I count it a privilege to write a word of introduction concerning him and his work.

Ever since Seminary days Wyn Blair Sutphin has taken the preaching office seriously, and has given himself to it with wholehearted dedication. This fact, combined with his great natural ability, has made him one of the most effective preachers in present-day America. His pulpit excellence has been recognized by his having a sermon included in the volume "Best Sermons," in 1955, and by his being invited to preach in some of the greatest churches in the western hemisphere—for example, Timothy Eaton Memorial, in Toronto, Canada. It has been attested even more strikingly by the eager response with which his ministry has met during the past five years in the First Presbyterian Church at Pompano Beach, Florida. There from small beginnings Dr. Sutphin has built up a great congregation; and recently a spacious and beautiful sanctuary has been erected to accommodate the thousands of worshippers who gather Sunday by Sunday.

These sermons on The Lord's Prayer, of which this volume consists, were preached in the regular course of Dr. Sutphin's ministry; but they have been revised for purposes of publication in book form. They well exemplify their author's Christian insight, gift of phrase, originality of form, and ability to make the Christian Gospel relevant to present-day life.

The late Dr. Willard L. Sperry, for many years the distinguished Dean of Harvard University Divinity School, once wrote this concerning The Lord's Prayer: "I know little in the Bible that bears thinking about quite as well." The readers of Dr. Sutphin's book—and I predict that there will be many—will realize afresh the truth of Dr. Sperry's statement.

NORMAN VICTOR HOPE

CONTENTS

9

THINE THE GLORY

I

THE PERFECT PARADOX

Our Father, Who Art in Heaven

Unlikely elements are joined together in the crucible of Christianity!

> Our faith is formed of paradox,
> composed of contradictions, seemingly divided,
> that unite about the character of God!

In Christianity the slave becomes the sovereign,

> and the grave becomes the womb of everlasting
> life.

What human mind could have conceived the contradictions of the manger?

> "Cold in His cradle the dewdrops are shining,
> Low lies His head with the beasts of the stall,
> Angels adore Him in slumber reclining,
> Maker and Monarch and Saviour of all!"

How does one reconcile the qualities of God's Omnipotence upon the one hand and His Immanence upon the other?

Is it possible that He can be aloof,

> and yet accessible?

Magnificent, and yet still mixed
with human elements?
The intimacy and
Infinity of God are, on the surface of it, inconsisten-
cies of faith.
We have to deal in double talk about divinity.
Of course, even the "prayer of prayers" addresses Him in dualis-
tic tone:
"Our Father, Thou who art in Heaven."
Near . . . but far,
predominant, but personal,
all things to all.
As Browning cried: "For thence, a paradox,
that comforts while it mocks!"
We have a dual divinity who is at once both infinitely
royal,

and yet intimately real.
Ah! Surely,
Infinitely Royal, hovering beyond the far end of the end of
man's intelligence!
One wonders at the people who go looking for the logic
in our faith.
Their lightning calculator minds click off the confines
of eternity,
and they apply the seismograph,
the litmus paper, and
the petri-dish in order to define Divinity.

They take the tool-kits of their intellects into the
stratosphere:

> the taperule,
> and the level,
> and the plumb line,

and then set themselves to trace the limitless topog-
raphy of God.

> It can't be done. You can't "inch-rule the
> infinite."

> "Canst thou by searching find out God?"

He cannot be compressed in creeds;

> He is not locked between the book ends;
>> He is not precipitated in a test tube;
>>> No, but "lost in wonder,
>>> lost in praise" we stand in
>>> awe of Him!

The only proof of God is God Himself!

> Like the eternal verities, He cannot be con-
> fined to measurements.

> You can't cramp courage into any category;
> you cannot take a Hooper rating of a person's
> faith;
> you cannot run statistical projections on
> affection;
> and you cannot make post-mortem on the thing
> called sacrifice.

Our faith is not a product to be analyzed; it's a
relationship to be enjoyed.

How many take itinerant and wayward jaunts at its
periphery!

"The real God," says the scientist, "is universal law, and once we bound the universe in its
successive layers, then we have identified
the Lord!"

As C. Day Lewis puts it in a poem:
"God is a proposition,
And we that prove Him are his priests,
His chosen,
From bare hypothesis
Of strata and of wind, of stars and
tides,
watch me construct His universe:
A working model of my majestic notions:
A sum done in the head.
Last week I measured the light:
His little finger.
The rest . . . is a matter of time."
"The real God," says the poet, "is a thing of
beauty and a joy forever." You will see Him in:
"The kiss of the sun for pardon,
The song of the birds for mirth,
One is nearer God's heart in a garden,
Than anywhere else on earth!"
"The real God," says the politician, "is Utopia."
His stock in trade is progress.
"Day by day in every way,

the world is getting better."
Buttons,
    bells,
        and buzzers play the grand
        concerto
        of our human progress!
    See! The course is upward and the race is to
    the swift!
So, men for centuries have turned the cannon barrels of
their telescopes to shoot the stars,
        have piled their paper calculations, file on
        file,
        have busied blackboards with their hodge-
        podge prophecies.
            But God, that "unknown element,"
            "that vast and baffling X," escapes
            them still!
Does it not comfort you to know you have a God beyond
your comprehension?
Have you never thought that if you knew all that there
is to know about Him, He could not be God?
Beyond His revelation there is still a mystery, an
"otherness," a God who is forever infinitely royal, and
                who rules the nations with
                a granite will.
    I like the thunder of His feet upon the earth!
    He sweeps His robes across its empires!

Aye, He speaks with lightning, and the
world obeys!
Perhaps you think that I exaggerate. You don't believe
He tumbles tyrants in the dust.

His hand is on the sparrow, but conspicuously
absent in our history.

Then let me ask:
Who ruled when Augustine was called
a saint?
Who was the king when Joan of Arc
was burned to cinder?
Who weeps today beside the tombs of
Charlemagne and Caesar, and
who lights the frenzied torches for
Il Duce and Der Führer? Who?

Rome had its day of power; within the century, its sun
had set.

Greece had its glory, which is gone,
Germany its boldness, blasted into
fragments now!
Indeed, who even knows the names that everybody knew in Jesus' time?

Who was the glamor-girl of old Galatia?
Who was the richest merchant in Jerusalem?
Who was the city manager of Corinth?
Tell me this: who was the idol of
the bobby-soxers in the town of
Bethlehem?

Who knows, who even cares?

But, twelve obscure and ordinary men, the first
disciples, are the world's extraordinary heroes!
Do not think that He has left the care and feeding of the
universe to amateurs! The Lord is not on a sabbatical.

However saturated with a rosy optimism, Browning's poetry is true:

"God's in His heaven,

All's right with the world!"

On January 16th, 1951, the church that I was
serving was destroyed by fire. In less than
fifty minutes it was down, and I was hanging
memories upon the skeleton that stood, and
mingling tears with ashes. When I rummaged
through the charred confusion, suddenly I came
upon a liturgy, face-downward, scorched about
the edges.

Let me tell you that it gives a man a
great security to take a sodden
liturgy and find it lying open to
the phrases:

"I believe in God,

Father Almighty,

Maker of heaven and earth!"

The Lord is Infinitely Royal: thence, a paradox, for He is also
Intimately Real.

"Our God," the prayer begins: someone we know.

We are not snagging stars along the route of some
ethereal excursion.

    We commence with certainties.

We won't be airborne on the flimsy wings of supposition;
    We shall start with substance.

When we come upon the Incarnation: *God made man,* we
stand before the first fact of our faith.

Here at this "Plymouth Rock" of Christianity, we come
upon the basis of belief:

> "The Word became as flesh,"
>
> Said Paul: "I know in Whom I have be-
> lieved!"
>
> We do not have a paper doll divinity, cut out of
> our imaginings, but real and robust; God comes
> down to man.
>
>   Ah, so!
>
> Our manifesto is a man,
>
> Our prayers are pointed toward a
> personality.
>
>   Make no mistake about it,
> our belief is not a welfare project,
> not a popular psychology, and
> not a pocket guide to better living.
>
>   It's a personal relationship with Christ!

I like the meat and bone of it!

This Christianity has weight and body, and it sets its
footprints on the centuries.

> It has a face like everyone's.

No, none of those formless generalities for me.
None of those academic postulations or poetic
rhapsodies.

    If God is God, then He must be iden-
    tified by something more than some
    obscure equations, or
        romantic legends.

I'm a blunt man, I confess, and some contrived
Divinity,
    some far-off gaseous illusion, cannot
    stir my soul!

To tell me God is something like: "the soul's
surmise,"
    a logical conjec-
    ture, or an
    ethical necessity,
    is saying, nothing!

Do not tell me that religion is a formula, or some
    anthology of tame, housebroken
    regulations.

That won't lift my loyalties to Heaven!
If Jesus *isn't* God; if, hovering beyond the
universe, a vast electric force discharges
the authority of God;
    if some dispassionate, impersonal
    mentality runs life through its
    eternal calculators;
    if my name is nothing but a whisper

on the wind, and
if my life is nothing longer-lasting
than a match flare scratched against the sky,
or else a short conjunction set between
two sentences;
if Jesus isn't God, why live?
In short, who cares *if* there's a God, unless we
can know *who*?
This God is one of us, and that makes all the difference!
When Christmas comes,
we do not fall before a test tube:
"for a formula is born,
and we shall call its name,
Wonderful Counselor, Mighty God!"
We do not bow before a document, and say:
"The Government shall be upon its
shoulders." No,
we do not give our lives unto a dream, some
gossamer suggestion, and affirm:
"The people that have walked in darkness see a light,"
But we drop down beside the manger, and we genuflect
before a switch of straw, and in the half light rub our
eyes at what we see: God in the flesh!

So, Augustine would write:
"He loves each one of us as though
there were but one of us to love!"

A German poet could cry out:
"My neighbor, God!"
Aye, that makes all the difference!
A little lad was lonely at his summer camp.
His parents hadn't written to him lately, and
he sent a frantic postcard to them. All it
said was:

"Mom and Dad:
I hope that you have not forgotten
where it was you put me!"
No, assuredly, He hasn't!

For, He shares our every circumstance.
He has been hungry,
lonely,
and deserted.
Often, He was tired.

He went by foot throughout the smallest villages
and knocked on any door.

He ate with sinners,
and He slept upon the open ground.
He went through everything you do.
No matter what your "via dolorosa,"
He has gone before.
His wayside Crosses mark the path.
Where no one cares, He comes.
Where no one travels, He is on the way.
Where all have fled, He takes a foothold.
Where the darkness settles, He will come

with candle and with cloak.

He is the only God who counts, because He is the only God
who cares!

Look you! He made no manuscripts,
            no money,
                and no monuments.

He sponsored no societies,
            and He endorsed no new detergents,
                and His world, when flattened
                out upon a map, is no more
                than a thumbprint smudged
                upon eternal time.

But we cannot forget Him; no, however much we
make a show of it!

I tell you: this itinerant evangelist upon a Cross was
nothing more than man, yet nothing less than God!

            As Browning put it:
        "It shall be
        A face like my face that receives thee; a man
        like to me
        Thou shalt love and be loved by forever;
        a hand like this hand
        Shall throw open the gates of new life to thee!
        See the Christ stand!"

A God both infinitely royal
            and intimately real:
                "Our Father, Thou who art
                in Heaven!"

With but a single breath a man can cry out:
> "Glory be to Thee, O God,"

and with the saint who said: "Closer is He than breathing and nearer than hands and feet!"
> One breath.

> For He is both at once, inseparable in contrast and united in division!

> Let me ask you, is God less than man?
>> Say, less than Whitman who once wrote:
>> "When I see a wounded person, I become the man,"
>> or less than Byron when he agonized:
>> "For I become a portion of that around me!"
>>> No! Although His Kingdom
>>> is eternity,
>>> His heart is yours!

In *Saint Joan* by George Bernard Shaw, Dunois, the soldier, is annoyed with her.
>> He breaks out in an angry speech:
>> "She trusts to God . . . she thinks she has God in her pocket!"
>>> Ah, I like the phrase!

> A king-sized God in pocket-sized edition!

> See: The King of Kings for every heart of hearts.

> "Our Father, Thou who art in Heaven!"

II

THE UNCOMMON DENOMINATOR

Hallowed Be Thy Name

There is nothing equal to the name of God in all the universe!
We set it reverently apart and keep it
special.
But, if you should say it isn't so, I'm prompted to agree
with you!
Have we not made the name of God a tool of
small household utility?
Have we not smudged it with the dirt of everyday?
And dragged it, face-flat, through the dust
of mediocrity?
Have we not set it down amidst the squalor
of indifference?
We take it as we take the daily round:
complacent,
nonchalant,
and unconcerned.
The glory has gone out of faith, and in its place a
sterile, antiseptic gospel goes off on its busybody
rounds.

Said Dr. John R. Mott some years ago:
"The trouble with the Christian faith today is
that we are producing Christian activities
faster than we are producing Christian faith!"
Ah, so!
Before the Name above all other Names
one ought to slump on bended knee!
"Thou shalt not take God's name in vain," the great
commandment says.
What does that mean: "in vain"?
It doesn't mean profanity. That's far too
small a sin to find a spot atop the ten best
sellers of all time.
But Dr. Elton Trueblood has deciphered it
with ease.
He says:
"It does not mean we are profaning or
rejecting Jesus' Name,
but taking it without a sense of
urgency or conviction!"
There you have it once again: "Don't take the
Name of God indifferently!"
We saunter up to Him with studied apathy,
as though He were the extra guest,
the uninvited,
or the odd man out.
The poet-preacher, Studdert-Kennedy has keened:
"They simply passed Him by,

They never hurt a hair of Him; they only let Him die.
For men had grown more tender, and they would not give
Him pain,
They only just passed down the street, and left Him in the
rain!"
We do that to the Name above all other Names!

No other in the universe can be so
Singular. It is a word not to be taken lightly:

to be mauled by indiscriminate mouthings,

nor to be mingled with the ordinary.

Dr. Frederick Norwood, once the minister of City Temple,
London, preached in New York fifteen years ago.
He talked about the Ten Commandments, and extemporized about his visit.
He was new to the United States, and he admitted his
naïvete.

"Thou shalt not take God's Name in vain,"
he said.
"Either you people in New York are all
exceptionally prayerful, or unbelievably
blasphemous. I walked behind two ladies
on Fifth Avenue, and with every other sentence,
one said to the other:

'My God Emma! My poor feet!' "

So, set apart? And separate?

To ancient peoples, names were magical.

The ancient Hebrews held Jehovah
in such awful reverence they

wouldn't write or speak the
Name of God,
and the original Old Testament is
spotted with respectful blanks.
The Catholics have organized a
"Holy Name Society" in order to
preserve God's sanctity!
Indeed, what do we do to keep it different?
How often Protestants profane the prayer:
"Hallowed by Thy Name!"
Some of our small religious sects or gross
commercialized evangelists have treated Jesus
with the same familiarity that breeds contempt.
As for the word, *ecclesia*, the church
bears small resemblance to the shabby and
decrepit thing that stands on side streets,
and goes stuttering in abject fear whenever
it is challenged by society.
Men have grown apologetic for the one thing
in the world that doesn't need apology!
Yes, Science, on your knees!
For each one of your blessings you
have brought a blight, and moral
infants fiddle with the universe.
You, too, Philosophy,
down in the dust!
With your "whatever works is right"
approach, you raise a family of

Frankensteins! and
You, Psychiatry, go hide behind the
skirts of guilt complexes and the
coattails of your self-expression, and
You, Government, whose snide manipula-
tions likely will maneuver us into the
holocaust of hydrogen destruction!
All of you, go grovel for forgiveness!
But, the universal church?
It is the body of the Lord Whose Name we hallow
at its altars!
But, unfortunately, many of its sanctuaries are
no more than meeting halls still sweating with
the boisterous fraternities of the community
and seldom fretted with ecclesiastical
adornments:
plain,
cold
and economical:
stern monuments to man's
lacklustre faith.
As for its program, when I see some busybody
church fuss-budgeting about statistics,
bristling with efficiency, and
buzzing with the hum of gossipy
good fellowship,
I want to cry: "Get to the business of
your belief!"

The church is not a clerical sweatshop where
we work our way into salvation!
Many of the services so often verge
upon vulgarity.
The Lord Almighty is addressed as though He
were the busboy, and the spoken prayers
backslap Him with a crackerbarrel chumminess.
Some clergymen, who never noted Pentecost, or
Trinity, or else Ascension Sunday,
are forever wringing wet with sentiment for
"Mother's Day," or celebrate "Be Kind to Our
Denominational Officials Sunday" every other
weekend!
If the congregations have been led up to
the altars of these secular occasions, who
can blame them if they've never heard about the
coming of the Holy Spirit, or the birth of
Jesus Christ into the human soul?
As for the preaching pastorate: it's openly
discounted, and the age of the Cathedral
Church and pulpit genius is almost gone.

> The modern church is chopped into
> suburban parishes,
> diminished into civic units,
> broken into fractured segments

and divided equally among the population!
So, today, the trend is toward the severed
church whose symbol is the hack and saw

           instead of Cross and Crown!

     Instead of studying to preach what men most
need to those who need it most,
           it splits God's gains and divvies
           up accounts.

So, even in the church, men have approached the King of
Kings with such offhandedness.

What do we do to keep God "different"?

There was, some months ago, a highly touted television
           program featuring a jazz recital in
           a church. All the advance publicity
           proclaimed, with sobbing throat and
           wetted eye, that it was dedicated
           to the memory of the composer's
           child, as though a noble motive
           might excuse ignoble work.

     Miss Dorothy Sayers, the late great theologian,
     puts it to us bluntly when she writes:
           "No piety in the worker ever compen-
           sates for work that is not true!"
           Indeed! Particularly, in the church,
           the worst cheat is a bungler,
           and the worst fraud is a botched-up job.
           The greatest blasphemy is shoddy work,
           the inexcusable is second-rate perfor-
           mance, and the crime above all other
           crimes is criminal neglect!
           Jazz in the church to hallow God?

How is that set apart and singular?
Here, in the holiest of holies, if we should admit
the honky-tonk,
> and barrel-house,
> then we defile the sanctuary!
Most music in most churches borders on the
blasphemous:
> the danceland tempos underneath the
> moonlight melodies.
There are too many chewing gum rhythms with
the tutti-frutti flavors:
> The saccharine sentimentalism of the
> romantic,
> and the open eroticism of the streets.
But there is music written only for the church
that has no counterpart outside:
> the corrugated roll of a chorale,
> the clean line of a plainsong.
How they separate us from the casual and the
extraneous!
Here in an age that bears the label, "nothing sacred,"
men must learn to keep Him Singular!
> "Hallowed by Thy Name!"
> No other in the universe is so
Superior. We have a strange perverted passion for equality
today.
> This is the hour of homogenized humanity.
> Split-level living is passé.

We reverence the ordinary.

Men are raising up a new ideal before them:
uniformity.

Whatever other people have applauded, they
approve.

We want to be the same.

Most people far prefer that to the expert and extraordinary.

If I point you to a dedicated intellect, who by
his choice is isolated from the world to solve
its limitations, the majority will say:

"He ought to be more human."

Never mind that he has lacerated space and cracked the
atom, if he isn't "chummy,"

if he doesn't "cuddle,"

if you cannot "chuck" him underneath the chin
or crack him on the back.

If he is not "hail fellow, ordinary
Joe," who does he think he is?

We have to live alike and like it. "Have you
never heard of

civic responsibility,
social adjustment?"

What are these? Arturo Toscanini,

Albert Schweitzer, and our
Saviour, Jesus Christ:
they never had them.
But today,

Instead of praying with the Pharisees: "I thank Thee,
Lord, that I am not as other men,"

> our blasphemy is more profound: "We thank Thee
> that we *are* as others are!"

> > Nobody better than the next!

Ah, so, we are set to it, aren't we? Everyone of us determined to be far more average than anybody!

> In Galsworthy's play, *The Mob*, the hero,
> Stephen, is a man who takes a stand against his
> government's tyrannical enslavement of a
> smaller nation.

> He refuses to be budged. Even his wife deserts
> him for the hue and cry. The common nature
> of her standard soul comes through. She says
> to him at last:

> > "You are very exalted, Stephen.
> > I don't like living,
> > > I won't live,
> > with anyone whose equal I am not."

> > How we insist on that!

So, every hobnailed yokel takes up the refrain: "I'm
just as good as you!" And even chants it at the altars
of the Lord!

> You see why many men can never hallow God.
> > They feel compelled to "equalize" Him:
> > to reduce Him to some small denominator;
> > call Him: "Teacher, friend, and all-

around good fellow, and that sort
of thing."
    But God Divine? "No, thank you."
In his Christmas oratorio, W. H. Auden has
a prayer supposedly composed by Herod. See,
he says,
"I asked for a God who should be as like me
as possible. What use to me is a God whose
divinity consists in doing difficult things
that I cannot understand? The God I want and
intend to get must be someone I can recognize
immediately without having to wait and see
what he says or does. There must be nothing
in the least extraordinary about him."

    But I tell you that He *is* extraordinary!
    Ah, what sets your soul to music,
    and what agitates your praises?
    Do you tremble at the lightning,
    riding like a razorback across the
    ribboned sky, or at the thunder
    crumbling up the heavens?
Let me ask: what dazzles you into devotion?
It is nothing when compared to Him!

    So, in a fanciful excursion
through his wishful thoughts, an author writes
about the people he would like to meet. He says:
"If Shakespeare were to come into the room,
we should rise to meet him, but if Jesus were

to come, we should fall down and try to kiss
the hem of his garment!"

"Hallowed be Thy Name."

There is nothing like to Thee, O Lord,

in earth,

or sky,

or sea!

III

LIVING LIFE INSIDE OUT

Thy Kingdom Come

We live perpetually in the present tense. Religion is especially
concerned with here and now.

Its kingdom is the small minutiae of the instantaneous,
the fingersnap of time,
the white flash of a second.
Its chronology is always the extemporaneous.
Its moments are forever,
its tomorrows are today.
"The Kingdom is," said Jesus, and He meant to say that
there is no division separating NOW and LATER.
Time is synchronized into the moment.
So, the person who intends to wait and see The Grand
Utopia will wait forever and he won't see anything!
Those chronological compartments we call
"history" and "destiny" do not exist.
The elements of time and space are
nonessentials to the faith.
The great verb in the Bible is the verb: "to be."
We always stand within the very midst of our eternity.

The hour *is* upon us. It is always "now or never" in
the Christian faith.

> Some years ago, I heard the writer,
> Sidney Montague, when he was speaking
> in Fort Lauderdale. Once, he had been a
> Northwest Mountie, and he told of how he had
> been lost up in the Rockies. He sat down in
> loneliness to write a poem, and entitled it:
>> "This Moment Is Forever!"

So, "the Kingdom" is the portable equipment of your life.

> It follows in the trail of Jesus, and he said,
>> "I *am* the Way, the Truth, the Life."
> He is the world's one lone contemporary!
> And at home in every age!

>> From oxcart to atomic rockets, He
>> has kept the pace!
>> You can't outdistance Him; He stands
>> before you at the end of every road!
>> You can't outrun His presence, for,
>> "He is in all our hurry and delay."
>> No, He has never left us for a moment,
>> and He never will!

> His dying breath will never be expired,
> His hand will never lose its hold,
> His final word will not be spoken,
> For He IS!

"There now," one wants to breathe in obvious relief,
"that puts life in a new perspective. No more castles

in the sky, nor manmade rearrangements of the universe."
When we pray, "Thy Kingdom come," we aren't post-
poning the event.
We are not setting clocks ahead to some apocalypse,
      nor stepping on an evolutionary escalator!
No, of course, I am not saying that religion is remote
from life.
We are to dress up in our Sunday glory and then walk into
the Monday world!
But the eternal kingdom is more than a social agency.
It does not bustle off to build a better world.
      None of that sanitized efficiency!
You are the kingdom, you, and not those pretty plans for
some envisioned paradise.

      The modern writer, Aldous Huxley, vents his
      venom in
      his novel, *Ape and Essence.* By his definition,
      progress is:
          "The theory that Utopia lies just
          ahead, and that ideal ends can justify
          the most abominable means; it is
          your privilege and duty to rob,
          swindle, torture, enslave and
          murder all of those who obstruct the
          onward march to earthly paradise!"
A better world? Beware of it, for life's reformers can
be cruel!
      John Calvin, founder of our faith, burned

Servetus because he disagreed.
The leaders of the Spanish Inquisition would
have told you with a perfectly straight face
that they were out to purify the kingdom;
and, of course, who can deny that Hitler hoped
to build a new Valhalla of the gods?
The kingdom isn't some dilapidated subdivision
of the universe,

> not some humanitarian development.
> The world will not be perfect.
> We have fluorescent bulbs; the heart
> is dark with sorrow.
> So, we have released the smallest
> element of life, but we have sent it,
> concentrated, into war.
> We understand the workings of the
> human mind, and yet the mental
> institutions bulge with sufferers from
> "man's own inhumanity to man."

An English paper put it well by saying:
"Man has conquered in the air, only to be
compelled to burrow underground."
So many people are deceived by progress.

> Never mind that Emerson once called it all,
> "Improved means to unimproved ends." Mankind
> is "on the up and up."
> His monuments span the rivers, cross the
> continents, and pierce the skies.

But I do not believe in them.

A snowflake is a monument to winter, but
it melts away.

A teardrop is a monument to sorrow, but
it dries.

The thunder is a monument to summer, but
it rolls away.

And so does progress.

It is all illusion and a breath can shatter it.

So many have obscured "the kingdom" by their private
causes.

They have called it:

"Civic betterment, or
forty-hour week, or
social justice."

"God the Father, Son, and Holy Ghost," was
rapidly replaced by a new Trinity entitled, "Food,
Clothing, and Shelter," and the new utensils of
the faith became:

The broom that makes a clean sweep,
and the soap-box that harangues the
multitudes; the survey that amasses
cold statistics, and the commissions
that interpret them, so that they
are incomprehensible!

Ah, but "the Kingdom," that
elusive glory, still escapes
them, for the kingdom is:

Within, and not without.

> It isn't some external circumstance, but an internal
> conviction.

> How does God, then, change the world? By changing *you!*
>> His monuments are men!

> Remember Jesus Christ Himself. Now, how did he attack
> the world?

>> You do not find Him jockeying for favorable
>> appointments.

>> He was never precinct leader for the party.

>> Though He saw men hungry and oppressed, He
>> didn't set up bread lines.

Yes, He was concerned, but no, He never treated the
externals; He got down to souls!

>> He knew that power never changes nature, only
>> places.

>>> It can only be transferred, but not
>>> transformed.

>>> What matter whether it be medieval
>>> despotism, or modern dictatorship?

You see, the point is this:

>>> "No rearrangement of bad eggs can make a
>>> satisfactory omelet!"

>>> It is the heart of man that counts!

What, after all, is history? Is it the cold, impartial
record of events, or is it heated by the warm biographies
of men?

Who can recall the party ticket Lincoln ran
upon? or
Who can name the war when Florence Night-
ingale began her work?

I tell you, history is men!
God's men and not man's methods move the
world!

When Dr. Cockburn of the Scottish
church once went to see a faithful
member, he was shocked to find him
very ill. He said he suffered.
While they talked together, suddenly
the man remarked with pain, "Ah,
minister, I tell you, when the heart
is wrong, then everything is wrong!"
The kingdom is within you, not without, and so
the problem is:

To get the inside out. That's how "the Kingdom comes" into
the world.

How does the inner grace become the outer force?
The answer is so simple that you won't believe it
at the first:

Be what you are.
"Beloved," wrote St. John, "we *are* the children
of the Lord."
Said Paul: "We have this treasure in earthen
vessels, always bearing about in our body
the dying of our Lord Jesus Christ!"

How many go at life the wrong side out and upside down!

Some years ago, a nearby colleague preached a
sermon with a most intriguing title that dis-
turbed me. It proposed the question:

"I'm in a Blind Alley. How Can I
Get Out of it?"

But I suspect that he arranged the cart before
the horse. The title should have been:

"I'm in a Blind Alley. How Did I
Get *Into it?*"

"Ah, minister,
I tell you, when the heart
is wrong!"

Start here, by *being* what you are.

How can I make this unmistakably apparent?

Take the church. Someone has said that "it is called
out of the world to minister unto the world." How true!

It does its best by *being* what it is:

a storehouse of divine imperatives,

a sanctuary from the shifting tides
of life,

a rehabilitation center for the
creaking centuries.

But, when it makes itself no more than just a
civic betterment auxiliary, or a chowder-and-
marching society, why, then by doing what it
shouldn't, it destroys its being!

Carlyle put it to us: "Make yourself an honest

man, and then you may be sure that there is one
less rascal in the world."

"Start here!". . . . be what
you are.
What better way to get our
inside out?

Examine race relations for a moment.

Would you thump the drum for integration?
Would you take the box and rouse the populace?
Indeed, there must be trumpets to the world!
But shouldn't you first, quietly, become a
brother in your own relationships?
Would you send monies off to teach the African
the love of Christ before you would consent to
kneel beside a Negro here at home? To do the
one without the other is a self-deception.

Geoffrey Studdert-Kennedy once said:

"The champions of the bottom dog
are only out to make him top dog, not
to make him a new man."

The fault of race relations is: you cannot
legislate the Kingdom. It must come from
inside out.

Or, take freedom of speech. That's controversial enough.

I can remember hearing of a most embarrassing
predicament of a Reverend McMasters. He was
preaching on the tale of Balaam and the
donkey that could speak. His title was too

literal, and appeared without the blessed benefit
of punctuation, so it said:

"Dr. G. P. McMasters The Ass That Talks."
But how would you defend his right to speak?
Would you align yourself with civil liberties
societies, or do you think the problem is
within?
The educator, Dr. Robert Hutchins, hits us
right on center. "Freedom of speech," he says,
"is empty unless *we have something to say!*"
Ah, there you have it! This is something deeper than mere
doing: be what you already are!

Nobody says it more succinctly than the poet,
Robert Frost:
"Make way for the one-man revolution, the only
revolution that is coming!"
For "the Kingdom" is
within you.

I am deeply tempted to propose: "The best way that you can
enrich society is to coin the metal you have in yourself."

Napoleon was in a rout as he retreated through
the Russian winter. Marshall Ney had volunteered
to lead the rear guard left behind to cover tracks.
It was a bloody business and certain death.
The army did come through, and some time later,
while the officers were at a table in the tent,
a blood-encrusted soldier fell inside.
"Who are you?" they asked.

"I'm Marshall Ney!"

They stared in disbelief.

"Where is the rear guard?"

And he pulled himself up to his height and
spoke deliberately.

"I am the rear guard!"

And *you* are!

When you kneel down to pray, "They Kingdom Come," include
the overture:

"O Lord, beginning now, with me!"

IV

UNDER NEW MANAGEMENT

Thy Will Be Done

Ironically, the most effective prayer is least employed.
    Most men avoid it as they would the plague.
        Instead of praying, "Lord, Thy Will be done,"
        they force their petulant
        demands on Him.
        They keep Him well-informed of every private
        whim and peccadillo,
        and they offer Him the benefit of their advice
        on everything.
    If everybody had his way, a million monkey wrenches
    would be thrust into the cosmological machinery, and,
    as the world went haywire, everyone could cry:
        "I got *my* way!"
Forcing our will on God is, literally, a universal pastime
in our prayers.
    Instead of wanting a religion that possesses us, we
    want a God whom we possess.
        Not even Jesus in Gethsemane had the audacity
        to order things His way!

"Let this cup pass . . . nevertheless, Lord,
not my will, but Thine!"

How many seek to bend Him to their will as though He
were a reed before the wind! They turn to Him for
special privilege, and at the taste of disappointment,
sour on Him once for all.

Our modern day has dragged Him after our desires as
though He were a flunky in a second-class hotel.

Man must be waited on!

How many make a laundry list of
personal demands and call it: prayer.

"I got stuck in Detroit," one minister said
from his pulpit, "but God got me out of it.
I had an airplane ticket in an hour.
I believe in prayer!"

Perhaps, but I do not believe his
story!

There is a kind of faith that works Him as a "good thing."

It believes He fidgets over us, and like a
mother hen goes clucking off on our appointed
tasks.

We curry favor in the courts of God!
We act as though we were ward-
heelers of the faith: each man a
private operator who expects to get
paid off in privilege.

I remember that one minister once went so far
as to engage a plane to circle Ebbets Field in

Brooklyn. This was in the Dodger days, and
from that soaring pulpit he announced that he
would make the prayers that would ensure a
Dodger victory! I have no sympathy with
that, for,

> in the first place, it's plain blas-
> phemy, and in the second, I was
> rooting for the Yankees!

Ah, you see! Instead of studying to know the will of
God, most men prefer to deify their own!

Said Dr. Pike, Bishop of California:

> "There's a tendency today to use God
> to enable us to get what we want to
> enjoy life as we would.
> True religion puts God first."

> I'm not alone in my suspicions.

Dr. Blake, the stated clerk of our denomination,
has agreed:

> "To try to use God for any purpose,
> however noble, is always wrong!
> 'Seek ye first the Kingdom,' not
> 'believe in the man upstairs,' and He
> will make you prosperous and success-
> ful."

Dr. Scherer, giant of the modern pulpit, has
accused this age of:

> "lobbying around in the courts of the
> Almighty."

Even His contemporaries used Him for a good
thing. J. B. Phillips translates Mark to say:
"they set out to take charge of Him!"
Indeed!
The long, long trek of history has marched beneath His
banner while it trampled out His cause.
He stands on every side of every issue; if
you trail His march across the pages of
man's history, you will discover He has criss-
crossed every line of demarkation.
Men have stamped His name on every
controversy, and have named Him sponsor
of their individual desires.
He has been labeled modernist . . . and . . .
fundamentalist.
Some claim He is a pacifist, and others put
Him at the head of militant revolts.
He is supposed to stand behind the Socialists,
while He is also linked with "laissez-
faire" free enterprise.
At both Republican and Democratic convoca-
tions,
He is listed as a member of the party.
See! The scalawags of destiny have held Him
as a hostage! He has been their "front man,"
posted at the head of every mean proposal.
In the era of the thirties, even
Communism has a party card for Him.

A poetess named Sarah Cleghorn penned a verse:

> "Ah, let no local Him refuse,
> Comrade Jesus hath paid His dues.
> Whatever other be debarred,
> Comrade Jesus hath HIS red card!"

I ride no hobbyhorse on this annoyance!

Even that old cynic, Shaw, once called the turn on us, when he referred to Christian practice as:

> "The gospel of getting on."

I tell you that the faith that only rings Him in emergency is worse than none at all; there is no sin so blasphemous as our religious arrogance!

The late A. Powell Davies put his tongue in cheek and poison in his pen when he revealed the charlatans for what they really are:

"Try God, folks! He will clear away your troubles in a twinkling! Works for you while you sleep. Works for you all the time. Cures your worries instantly! Nothing for you to do. And so inexpensive. Remember the name, folks! GOD! Go to your corner church today, folks, and get God! G O D, easy to pronounce, easy to remember, easy for you in every way. Try God! This program is brought to you by

Self-Interest and Vulgarity, Inc., with
branches all over America. Remember, folks!
Try God!"

This prayer, "Thy Will Be Done,"
demands:

Your Undivided Life.

How many souls are torn upon the bloodlands of internal strife!

Did you see Robert Sherwood's drama on the life of
Lincoln?

In a moment of excruciating indecision, Abe
blurts out:

"You talk about a Civil war; there
seems to be one going on inside me
all the time. One of these days I'll
just split asunder and part company
with myself, and it'll be good rid-
dance from both points of view."

How many men extemporize in trivia, and
squander life as though it were of small account.
They spill themselves, like shivering quick-
silver, and run off in small distractions.
Stephen Leacock once described them in an essay
when he sketched a character:

"He mounted horse, and then rode off
in all directions!"

Ah! So many lives are runaway and go off
galloping down every avenue of casual desire,
and racing after every pandering emotion.

Day by day, the snip-snip of the insignificant
trims them to size.
They fiddle-faddle life away upon some honkey-
tonk desires.
The slightest, most minute, distraction drains
their energies away on fripperies and fads.
They give their lives up to the finical and
trifling, and at the last, their whole horizon will
have been no larger than the most immediate
necessity and casual frivolity!
This is the waste most wicked in the world!
I say to you: the most lamentable of losses is
the loss of energy!
So many men are spendthrift with themselves!
They break their brittle lives into the fractures
of futility.
You hear it said of them:
"They have too many irons in
the fire!"
They burn up life with small explosions
of enthusiasm, and you know the type:
they're always cutting ribbon on a new beginning
day of enterprise.
They live amid the rubbleheap of half-accom-
plished causes:
things half-done,
hopes half-built,

and dreams half-baked.

The wasted life!

A poet wrote:

"Once I read about a man who was tied
down and the ants ate him.

I am tied down, too, and little things
are eating me:

The friend who calls me on the phone
and talks and talks,

The agent who is determined to sell me
a mop,

The children who quarrel and will not
do their lessons,

The letters that must be answered before night, somehow.

All these things are devouring me alive.

My eyes cannot see, my ears cannot hear,

Even my brain is being destroyed.

Only the husk of me smiles wearily on
and on."

Most wicked!

Most profane!

Most blasphemous!

What do men think they are? A bauble of no consequence,
that they so easily and smugly squander everything they
are on anything at all?

For this, the Christus bleeds, and God bows
down to weep!

How different when life is gathered up, drawn in around the center and united at the footboard of the Cross!

The magic word of life is ONE.

When life becomes a fraction, you are finished!

Somewhere minds have got to be made up! You cannot be half-Christian any more than you can be

> half-born, or
> half-alive, or
> half-content.

Consider prayer. It never works unless you are resigned to it.

As long as there are qualifying clauses and restrictions, then there is refusal.

And so many prayers are tagged with some conditions.

There's a "rider" snagged on to the proposition.

There's a "catch" in it.

St. Augustine once prayed: "Lord, save me from my sins! (All except one)."

God answered that parenthesis, and left him to his own device.

And then he prayed: "Lord, save me from my sins (but not quite yet)."

God answered the condition. He avoided him.

At last he prayed: "Lord, save me from my sins!"

And then God grasped them by the scruffs
of their unsanitary necks and stamped
them out!
You cannot pray a half-a-prayer to ask
for half-a-blessing from a half-a-God!
I can remember hearing Dr. Fosdick preach upon the
subject:

"On Getting One's Self Off of
One's Hands."

Lord, how we wish we could!

Try giving everything you are to all
that matters:
Jesus Christ!
No matter, then, what battlegrounds
you must go out upon,
no matter where, you cannot lose!
Though bleeding, you are
never broken.
Though weary, you are never weak,
though driven, you will never
see defeat!
If you should fear to go that far in
faith, remember, then,

God's Undefeated Law.

The reason most of us restrain ourselves is that our nose
are too short and we can't see beyond the end of them.
"How can you say His way is winning out," you

ask me, "when it isn't? Trust Him and surrender
to Him? Well, I just don't dare! I can't
discern Him in the heavens ruptured with explo-
sives and dirtied with atomic offal, nor discover Him within a universe that pirouettes
upon a precipice! How can you say He rules?
God's undefeated law, indeed!"

Indeed, the Ultimate is
always His!

I do not bring to you a hokus-pokus word of prestidig-
itation:

no snap of the fingers and, *Voilà!*—
Utopia!

The world is never any worse or better than it is
this moment.

There is no progressive evolution, hauling
us into a perfect time-to-be.

What made you think that happiness was everybody's
birthright? And whoever said it was the normal state
of being?

That's a celluloid prevarication rigged by
Hollywood.

The curtain comes down on another happy
ending,

and the music mounts up to crescendo!

Ah, but life is lived off-stage, behind the
scenes, and suffering is written in the script
of it!

So, even Christianity had its concep-
tion on a Cross,
its birth within a tomb,
its childhood in its persecutions!
No, religion doesn't "get you off" from life. There are
no special cases and emergency exceptions. No,
the will of God was not suspended for the Christ
Himself!
I ask you: were the nails of rubber, and the
sponges saturated with a *rosé* wine?
Now, was it really blood he bled, or some
symbolic, false facsimile? Or,
Was it really raining rain at all, or only
violets?
Of course He suffered, and may I remind you that the
martyrs went out to their scaffolds and arenas without
anesthesia!

What did you expect?
Says Dr. Elliott of Texas:
"People think religion is a kind of
rabbit's foot. There is no basis for
that in the whole New Testament.
Christianity is no sentimental
first aid kit!"
Ah, so! Well, what did you expect from a
religion born, like old Br'er Rabbit, in a
briar patch?

Look at Jesus! Trouble was His stock in
trade,
    disaster was His destiny,
        pain was His only pride!
I say to you: you cannot petticoat that
portrait with a rosy optimism without dese-
crating God! There's no immunity in Christianity!
    Life's greatest lessons must be
    learned by ruler-rap.
The school of hard knocks is in constant
session, and the black and blue are hoisted
as the colors of experience. We get to know
that one way or another; we must all mount
Crosses if we are to wear the Crown.
This is the sad lament of Dr. Fosdick in his
sermon titled: "What Is Vital In Religion."
    "Why is it," he has written, "that
    some of life's most revealing in-
    sights come to us not from life's
    loveliness, but from life's diffi-
    culties? Why are all the vitamins
    in spinach, and not in ice cream
    where they ought to be?"
He works His will through suffering.
    If you remember back, you learned the most
    from knuckle-raps, and not from lollipops.
Your infantile disasters made a mark on you.

There was a day in my own life when my mater-
nal uncle dragged me through the streets to
meet the village bully who had taunted me
that morning. I remember that my uncle told me,
harshly, when I wouldn't go alone, that if the
bully didn't beat me, then *he* would, for he
would never stand a coward in the family.
I thought my uncle hated me that moment; but
I went with him,

>   *and I won,*

and I have never been the same since then!
Ah, so with God.

>   The outcome spells success!

>   The ultimate is victory!

>   He cannot be defeated at the last!

You see, you cannot make life easy for the simple reason
Jesus came to make men strong.

>   "Whom the Lord loves, He corrects."

>   The world's best saints have been its sorriest
>   sinners;

>   its greatest healers, once its most afflicted;

>   its gentlest saviours, once its most abused!

What I am putting to you plainly is the proposition:
even when the will of God seems difficult, give it your
undivided life!

>   My soul, how sensible that is!

>   Now, obviously, everybody has to suffer, and
>   the only question is: "For what?"

For, if you do not suffer in a noble cause,
you suffer blindly, stupidly, and in a dumb show.
Nothing is more pitiful than pain that has no purpose.
When anything so terrible as agony is wasted,
it's a double tragedy!
An army surgeon had to amputate a soldier's
arm in World War II. He never hardened to
the job, and dreaded to go in the ward to
break the news. After the operation, he walked
in to find the boy white-faced and conscious,
and he said in sympathy,

"I'm sorry that you had to lose
your arm."
The boy protested, feebly:
"But, I didn't lose my arm; I *gave* it!"
So, even then, when life comes tum-
bling in, when all the chips are down,
and everything is riding on
a prayer,
don't be afraid to place yourself beneath
His management.

Remember, it was Paul, not Pilate,
who was beaten,
Christ, not Caesar, who was on
the Cross!

V

ALL OR NOTHING AT ALL

Give Us This Day

The most misunderstood of prayers is the petition for the small
necessities:
>"Give us this day our daily bread."
It seems so insignificant a cry:
>the interruption of a triviality,
>the imposition of the picayune.
Examined as it stands before us, it's a mean proposal
on a beggar's tongue.
Is ours a "trick or treat" belief in which we ring Him,
with a sack for goodies?
Is it God's eternal welfare project: every man a
slugabed free-loading on the universe?
Is our belief dependent on a well stocked larder?
Is the symbol of the faith the horn of plenty . . .
or the empty Cross?
You answer that, because you ought to know!
Some charlatans and fakers have been touring the religious
circuit with the odious proposal that
>"religion pays!"

You ought to scramble to it, not because its Saviour
sacrificed Himself,

        but, frankly, for the reason that it helps
        us to success.

Some of them tell us how to be successful and serene, forgetting,
    in the heat of rhetoric, that Jesus fitted into neither
    category!

Is our faith no more than manna in the desert,

        breakfast on the table,

        and a chicken in the pot?

I understand that missionaries meet this niggardly,
negotiable faith on every field.

They have their "bread and butter" Christians.

It's impossible to count the converts in some mission
stations, till the soup lines are abandoned and the
truth is out!

        The ranks thin down,

        the stragglers sound retreat,

        and what is left, when persecution,

            isolation,

            and starvation are the horsemen

            of the hour;

        what is left we call the church.

This is a statement of assurance.

    We do not expect to be spoon-fed and wet-nursed through-
out life!

    It's not a dowdy little prayer for table scraps;

    but it's a ringing affirmation of the rulership of God.

It's much more of an attitude than supplication,
and its value is as a reminder
rather than a requisition.
It assures us He is "all or
nothing" in our lives.
You cannot keep Him "in His place," because He has no place
but yours.
In every area of life, He stands supreme!
A lot of people think religion should be vacuum-packed
and watertight.
They think that we should "keep religion in its place,"
and their belief is, literally, "out of this world":
fashioned out of fantasy,
and sketched against a cloud bank with
the air brush of a free imagination.
"Keep to your cubbyhole," they say,
"don't interfere."
One wonders how they reconcile that with the character
of Christ:
"Remember me to that old fox," He said
of Herod,
"Generation of vipers," He called
the Pharisees,
"A den of thieves," He cursed the
money-changers.   .
Aye, He nosed about in everybody's business.
He had a bone and blood existence.
No, the Master wasn't some translucent

substance sent out of the "nowhere" to
the "now", for plainly, He was not oblivious
of life.

He chose it for his battleground,
and he accepted its encumbrances.
So many men employ the witchery of words in order to confuse.
They draw up a dividing line between the sacred and the secular
and call them different.

"Don't dirty faith," they say, "by rubbing it in life.
No, keep it to the incensed altar and the lilied bower
lest it smell of man's mortality."

It is a subtle trickery.

You see: the sacred—and—profane,
the spiritual—and—the worldly,
the religious—and—material.

Life splits in two, and God
becomes a half-a-God who only
rules the half of life!

Religion is confined to church and cloister:
when "the worship's over, God returns
to Heaven,
and stays there until next Sunday
at eleven."

There is a fine finesse at work!
One cannot help but to admire the skilled adroit-
ness of a master hand!
Sacred AND secular! Imagine that!

As though God could be boarded off
into compartments,
As though men could cry to Him:
"Keep off . . . no trespassing."
Somebody ought to tell them they've been taken!
Do they not live in the universe: ONE world?
Whose physical geography
and private urges
were the Master's own inventions?
Spiritual on one side and material upon the other?
Is there any difference?
Are they not, in fact, identical?
No, there is nothing wrong with matter. After all,
God made it. Do you, then, accuse God of
an evil thing?
Take money. I am not against that. There are
just two kinds of people who despise it:
fools and madmen.
But, there is nothing wrong with it.
I like it. And one thousand dollars
consecrated in the stone and mortar of
a church becomes a spiritual thing.
Now, what are bread and wine? They are
the coarse materials of life.
Lift but a palm in blessing, and
they are the sacraments: God's
flesh and blood!
What is water? It is but a bland necessity.

Go dip the fingers into it and it
becomes the Jordan, rinsing off our
sins.

The sacred AND the secular?
Insidious inventions of the devil,
that do not exist in fact.

There is nothing more "religious" in a pot of incense
than there is within a bonfire of September leaves.

I think that Dr. Fosdick dressed it in dramatic
language when he said:

"We Christians build an ecclesiastical
ghetto into which we have put Christ!"

Apart from life!

One summer on vacation we were visiting a
large and influential church.

Upon the altar was a jewelled cross imported
from the Orient. I noticed that on week days
it was covered with a flannel sack.

It was a gruesome sight.

I wondered why, and I inquired about it:

"Surely," I began, "the church is
not in mourning."

"No," was the reply, "we cover it
to keep the dirt away."

Imagine! "A protected cross!"

What sermons could be spawned from that!
Our faith is not a guarded sanctuary from
the world.

> The moment that you run to it, you stand out in
> the midst of life,
>> For life is where it lives!
>
> When someone joins the church so many parishes confuse
> the issue.
>> They immediately set about recruiting the
>> reluctant souls into committee workers,
>>> canvassers,
>>> and amateur evangelists.
>
> "You ought to be about some Christian service!"
>> The insidious assumption is that all the rest
>>> of life is basically unworthy.
>>> So, at last, a first-rate mother,
>>> or a topnotch carpenter is dissipated
>>> into so-called "spiritual" work.
>> What is more pleasing to the Lord than honest
>> occupation? Have you turned a Christian?
>>> If you are a butcher, give an
>>>> honest weight!
>>> a housewife? Make your husband's
>>>> life a thing of joy!
>>> a dentist? drill it clean and
>>>> oh, God love you,
>>>> drill it painlessly!
>> He enters into all of life or none at all.
>>> "Give us this day."
>>> And, too, this prayer assures
>>> us that:

*You cannot have religion when you need it, if you didn't have
religion when you didn't need it.*

You can never tag it "for emergency"
               or "just in case."
It's something good to know about, in case
it's true.
It's wise to have one more "ace in the hole"
if things go wrong.
It's clever of us to hold something in sus-
pension for a later time.

               Ah, no! You cannot have
                       the victory without the
                       skirmish,
                       the prize without the contest,
                       nor the crown without the cross!

This is a firm and steady prayer: "Give us
this day."

               It's not the frenzied howling of the
               desperate, nor the greedy wheedling
               of the self-indulgent.

No, it pulls no rabbits from a hat.

               It isn't done with mirrors.
                       There is nothing in the
               Christian life that is accomplished
                       by the mere snap of a finger,
                       or the waving of a wand.

He is the Saviour of the world and not its
sorcerer!

The words He made immortal on the
mountainside were not:
> "abracadabra,
> presto-chango,
> and *voilà!*"

As I remember them, they had to do with everyday realities: hard words with rough-hewn edges:
> "Crucify,
> rise up,
> and follow after!"

Prayer is not an open hatch to some
accommodating generosity.

You cannot have it when you need it, if you
didn't have it when you didn't need it!

Ah! too easily a man abandons faith!

Give us the leaf upon the bough,
> The fruit upon the vine,
> > The froth upon the wave;

Give us the chime of laughter ringing on the air,

Give us all these, and we can keep our confidence
alive!

But, let the dark days hang their draperies
across the heavens,

let the empty corridors of loneliness return
our voices to us, void, and

let the wind come fumbling in the gullies of
our lives for our discarded dreams,
> and resolution slackens once again!

What has it been in your life?

Grief? Were you so foolish as to go down to the "valley
of the shadow" all alone?

You should have taken "rod and staff."

"They comfort me."

Or failure? Did you have amnesia of faith so that you
didn't think of Jesus

who was scalded by the mockery of men, and
skewered to a cross?

Or loneliness? Did someone walk out on your life and
leave the bare walls echoing so loud with memory you
couldn't hear the old refrain:

"Lo, I am with you always, even to the end?"

It doesn't matter, does it, what it was?

It was a tragic thing to take you from
your God!

In all of life, He's all
that matters.

Aye, the day will come when you will not
know where to turn

unless you have already turned
to Jesus Christ!

VI

THE QUALITY OF MERCY

Forgive Our Sins As We Forgive

In *Major Barbara,* the playwright, Shaw, protests:
"Forgiveness is a beggar's refuge . . . we must pay
our debts!"
The poet, Heinrich Heine, once dismissed his sins with
debonair abandonment:
"God will forgive me," he insisted, "it's His business!"
How many men reiterate: "To err is human,
to forgive divine," as though
it were compulsory and categorical.
In his Christmas Oratorio, the poet Auden, says
it more succinctly:
"Every crook will say:
'I like committing crimes, God likes
forgiving them!
The world is admirably arranged!' "
Indeed, it seems, on sight, to be a simpleton's solution:
"Eat and drink, and then be merry!"
"Burn the candle at both ends, and then blow
the smoke into the face of God!"

Why not? It's no skin off our teeth,
for when the reckoning comes round,
we sign it with a flourish, 'Jesus Christ,'
and like a soft, indulgent Father, He
will settle the account.
        "A beggar's refuge?"
Ah, far worse than that! A scoundrel's
license!
Frankly, have you never thought religion let you
off too easily?
Or, has it not offended you to find some sodden
derelict dismissing forty years of wallowing
depravity with the insolent presumption:
        "I've been saved!"
        It sounds so easy!
        Almost too good to be true!
        And let me tell you that, assuredly,
        it is!
Of course, God's love is always open-end.
        Now, mind you, Jesus never turns in to the wall.
        He stands face-forward to the world of men.
        When did he ever say, "Depart from me?"
                Where did you read that Calvary was
                staged exclusively for the preten-
                tious few?
                He knew the world's most filth-encrusted
                criminals: the lot of them, unappetizing and

repulsive, grubby little creatures with the
manners of a boxcar
and the morals of a rabbit hutch.
If you should calculate the sum of their
perversities you would have an itemized account
of every variation on an ancient theme.
But not once, anywhere, does Jesus say:
"I sicken at the sight of you!"
"The love of God is broader
Than the measure of Man's mind.
And the heart of the Eternal
Is most wonderfully kind."
Ah, so! But God is not a dupe. He doesn't let us off
"scot-free."

Murdo MacDonald put it well when he proposed
that "Ours is a religion that hurts!"
Indeed it does! Christ on a cross is not a
stereopticon illusion, and
Forgiveness is a hard experience!
God forgives you, and it is His business.
In fact, as Dr. Reinhold Niebuhr scores it:
"Only the infinite mercy of God can meet the
infinite pathos of human life!"
But it is *not* a "beggar's refuge." Let me tell you
that you pay for it.
In the economy of God, forgiveness is a
premium commodity.

It hurts to ask for it.

In case your sense of fair play is offended at the
thought of "socialized" compassion, free to anybody
for the asking, then remember in your life how often
you petitioned someone for forgiveness.

> You could count the times upon the fingers
> of one hand!

> > Admitting you were wrong!
> > Lord, how it hurt!

> A man will do most anything in order to
> avoid it.

See! The cowardly contraptions that we rig in order
to conceal ourselves!

> Most of the mental maladjustments of mankind
> are due to the distortion of his sense
> of guilt.

> > A man must hide his sins.
> > Perhaps he blames somebody else for
> > them, and that is "paranoia,"
> > or, conveniently, retreats into
> > another personality and that
> > is "schizophrenia."

> Forever playing hide-and-seek, he'd rather lose
> his faculties than face up to himself!

So, we avoid our sins by name, and sheath them in
sophisticated language.

We have decorated every vice to look like virtue.

Every grubby soul goes by some alias.

"Semantics! Bring me words to hide myself!
Teach me the trickery of terms!"
So, sin arrives incognito and
                    speaks sub rosa.
One can hardly recognize it as
          "delinquency," (that sounds so harmless), or, as
          "complex," (and now anybody who is anybody
          ought to have one!),
          or a
          "misdemeanor," (just a simple slip of small
          concern).
A man is called uncultured,
          crude and
                    coarse,
if he should mention our monstrosities by title and
then classify them by the gut and groin.
We wear the papier-mâché mask of piety, and preen ourselves with "pretty polly" talk of innocence.
          Small wonder Hamlet railed against the
          pleasant face his uncle put upon an illegitimate
          relationship,
                    "O villain, villain, smiling,
                    damned villain!
                    My tables! Meet it is I
                    Set it down,
                    That one may smile, and smile,
                    and be a villain;
                    At least, I'm sure it may be so

in Denmark!

So, uncle, there you are!"

That finger-thrust is at our throats! Have we
not lied in them in order to prevent the sentence:

"I was wrong, forgive me!"

"What a tangled web we weave

When first we practice

to deceive!"

Indeed, a man will go to any length to keep from the
humiliation of the Cross.

Some time ago I chanced upon a sermon that
denied all human guilt as "unhistorical,

unscientific,

and unbiblical."

That's wishful thinking at its most fantastic!

Let me ask you: "Why did Jesus die?"

Because he was a rabid revolutionary?

Or insipid vagrant?

Or a public nuisance?

Did he die for some ennobling proposition like:
"All men have been created equal"?

Did He fall into the dust because He was a dupe:
a disillusioned hero who had "had enough"? Or
did He die for you because you aren't the man
you think you are?

Who would outsaint the saints?

Who would outrank them in their

righteousness,

outshine them in surrender, and
outface them in
their faith?
Then hear them in their own confessional!
Not one of them once boasted of his virtue,
or went strutting with the braggadocio
of smugness.
Peter wept because he was so vacillating he
denied the Christ.
"Depart from me," he cried, "I am a sinful man."
St. Paul said this: "I am the chief of sinners!"
David, poet of the Hebrews, sobbed: "Create in
me a clean heart."
See, the saints at eventide who kneel to pray:
"O Lord, be merciful to me a sinner!"
Aye, confession may be beneficial to the soul, but it
plays havoc with our vanity!
It hurts to see the thing that we have done!
How like the chaplain in the play, *Saint Joan,*
when he came hurtling from the horror he had
seen, the odor of the sizzling flesh caught
in his throat. He cried:
"When you have *seen* the thing that you
have done,
when it is blinding your eyes,
stifling your nostrils,
tearing your throat, then . . .
O God! take away this sight from me!"

Indeed, you earn forgiveness by the asking of it!
For it is, by far, the spirit's most excruciating prayer:

"O Lord, be merciful to me, a sinner!"

So, forgiveness hurts!

It hurts to give forgiveness,

and the only sentence harder than: "I'm sorry," is:
"You are forgiven."

Jesus wrenched it out of death!

If you are Christian, you are in the red, and

the account is written in the blood of Christ!

Wherever you have found the words, "Forgive them," you
have found a Cross!

There is an ancient legend often told about
the Prodigal. You know that it was dusk when
he returned back to his doting father. So,
the celebration was illuminated by the lamp-
light, and the night was dim. The next day
through the next, the Prodigal slept on.
At last, when he awoke, he looked out in the
sunlight to the old familiar fields, and saw
his father working. It was then he noticed
for the first time that his *father's hair*
had turned completely white!

Lord, how it hurts . . . just to forgive!

I hope you notice this reciprocal requirement of the
prayer.

We ought to set its house in order by a
rearrangement:

> "Lord, as we forgive, forgive
> our sins."

In World War II, the English writer, C. S. Lewis,
advocated the forgiveness of the Nazis.
"Everybody says forgiveness is a lovely idea,"
he wrote, "until they have something to forgive.
And then, to mention the subject at all is to
be greeted with howls of anger. . .
'That sort of talk makes them sick,' they say.
And half of you already want to ask me,

> 'I wonder how you'd feel about for-
> giving the Gestapo if you were a Pole
> or a Jew?'

So do I! I wonder very much. I am not trying
to tell you what I could do. I can do precious
little. I am telling you what Christianity is.
I didn't invent it. And, there, right in the
middle of it, I find,

> 'Forgive us our sins as we forgive,
> those who sin against us.'

There is not the slightest suggestion that we
are offered forgiveness *on any other terms.*
It is made perfectly clear that if we don't
forgive, we shall not be forgiven!"

> Did we ever say it sounded, once,
> so easy?

Ah, most difficult and most demanding!
For, between the open-armed, embracing mercy
of the Lord,

>there stands this pettifogging soul
>of man that cannot get its small
>hostilities out of its craw, nor
>neutralize the rancor in its heart!

Unless we can forgive, we cannot be forgiven!
Ah, that hurts!

As for the quality of mercy, it is strained!

>George Eliot knew that when she wrote
>*Adam Bede.* It is the tragedy of tainted
>life. Adam, the hero, was in love with
>Hetty with an honest, clean affection.
>Arthur Donnithorne, however, took the
>heedless girl and wrecked her life. At last,
>when everyone is hopelessly unhappy,
>Donnithorne repents and comes to Adam for
>forgiveness. It is far too late to make
>things up, but Adam gives his hand in mercy,
>and he says:

>>"But, there's a sort of damage,
>>sir, that can't be made up for.
>>Aye, you whose sin hurts other
>>people, you remember that!"

>>Remember that!

One time an angry man protested to
John Wesley:

"I *never* forgive!"

The answer Wesley gave him was:

"Then, sir, I hope you never sin."

When someone odious offends you;

when you drink the wine of sour grapes,

and tramp the vintages of wrath;

when you are burdened and harassed,

don't waste your own eternal soul on grievances!

"He drew a circle that kept me out:

Heretic, rebel, a thing to flout;

But love and I had the wit to win.

We drew a circle that took him in."

Forgiveness hurts.

It hurts to accept it.

It's a strange perversity that sits forever in perpetual
self-judgment.

It's a rare conceit that makes itself the prisoner at
every bar, and the condemned at every hanging.

But, there are some people like that, and you know them.

God has long ago forgiven them, but they cannot forgive
themselves.

Like Buddha staring at his navel, they are
fascinated by their guilt!

They cannot keep their eyes from it!

The Reverend Lyman Hartley, Senior,
pioneered as Chaplain of the Presbyterian
Hospital in New York City, and he told us,
several years ago, about a patient who had

been referred to him because she was dis-
gusted with herself. She had been guilty
of immoral conduct. The psychiatrists had
analyzed her and revealed the causes, but
her soul was sick and nauseated.

What she said to him was:
"Reverend, I know the reason I
have sinned, and I have stopped
the sinning, but I can't forgive
myself!"

His answer took her by surprise.
"What right have you," he said,
"to keep in judgment on yourself
once God already has forgiven you!
You have no right to contradict Him.
You are free!"

How like the ancient saying: "One
ought never to remember what the
Lord is willing to forget!"

Aye, let the dead past turn to ashes. What is done is
done, and He will cover our mistakes with mercy.

"Look, Father, look on His anointed face,
And only look on us as found in Him.
Look not on our misusings of Thy Grace,
Our prayer so languid and our faith so dim,
For, Lo, between our sins and their reward,
We set the passion of Thy Son, our Lord!"

Forgiveness isn't easy, after all. It's hard to ask for, and to give, and to accept.

But, life without it is a life condemned.

Sir J. Y. Simpson first used
anesthesia in childbirth. He was asked upon
his death bed what had been his great
discovery
and he replied, of course,

"That God forgives."

VII

TINKERING WITH TRAGEDY

Lead Us Not into Temptation

God doesn't work against Himself.

He doesn't play both ends against the middle, alternately
leading us into temptation, and then riding to
the rescue.

He is not responsible for evil, secretly engaged in a
malevolent collusion with the enemy.

It's not God's fault we sin.

He doesn't push us into it and say: "Go to!"

The Lord is Holy, and He cannot countenance the mere
flick of an innuendo.

How, then, can we pray: "Our Father, lead us not
into temptation?"

And the answer is: of course, we can't.

The Lord's Prayer never slumped into the
sorry posture of this wheedling and defamatory
sentence.

In the Greek the verb is not: "to lead," but,
"to allow."

That puts the whole responsibility for sin where it

belongs, upon the free, unfettered will of man, and
says, then, in effect:

"Dear Lord, keep us from gambling
with our souls. Don't let us take a
flyer after every casual desire.
Do not let us experiment with evil."

No more tinkering with tragedy: Russian roulette
with all the chambers loaded!

It's a way of saying: "Let us see the way the
cards are stacked, and the shells are shuffled.
Don't let anyone be taken in. Do not let us
experiment with evil."

Ah, how sensible, for, in the first place, let it now be
said of evil, that:

The more we practice it, the less we know about it.

One could parody an ancient phrase and say that "prac
tice makes imperfect."

No one knows so little about evil as the man who most
performs it.

C. S. Lewis, with his surgical precision,
cuts us to the core:

"When a man is getting better, then
he understands more clearly the evil
that is in him. When a man is getting
worse, he understands his own badness
less and less. *A thoroughly bad man
thinks that he's all right!*"

Indeed! It is the nature of all evil to disguise itself!

What did you think? That it would come announced?
>   When did you last see sin in technicolor, adver-
>   tising in advance, and pasted up with placards
>   to identify it?
No, you never have.
>   Real sin is subtle.
>   It protects its name.
>   It builds a reputation in the town.
− It gets on as a "good thing" for the whole
community.
>   Most sin is average and normal.
>   At its most insidious, it seems most
>   innocent, and it is far more likely
>   to be found behind the veil than
>   underneath the rouge.
Do not imagine that the devil is a bumpkin.
>   Shakespeare pegged him to the proper hook when
>   he suggested that
>   >   "The Prince of Darkness is a
>   >   gentleman!"
Indeed, and Shakespeare recognized the devil's
way with men. *Richard the Third* revealed the
subtle, sly technique:
>   >   "And thus I clothe my naked villainy
>   >   With odd old ends stolen out of
>   >   holy writ;
>   >   And seem a saint, when most I play
>   >   the devil."

Crafty!
Snide!
And Shifty!

Did you once imagine you could outmaneuver
anything so slippery, or you could "play it
cagey" with that old manipulator?

Would you, then, experiment with evil?
Then beware!
The more we practice it, the less we
know about it.

Nothing in this life is so distorted as the face of evil!

In our time, the Seven Deadly Sins are openly
commended everywhere.

If custom is criterion, and
performance definition, then they
should be labeled:
virtues.

We have learned the artifice of Pharisees.
We dress them in the cap and greaves of our
theatrical deception. With a histrionic flare,
we put a clean face on a dirty thing:

So, *Lust* is called, "majority behavior,"
Wrath is camouflaged as "righteous
indignation,"
Greed is recommended by the name of
"thrift,"
Our *Gluttony* is advocated as "planned
obsolescence,"

> *Laziness* is palmed off as "neutrality," and
> *Envy* passes as "equality,"
> And *Pride* comes costumed in the sock and
> buskin of "success."
>> So easy!
> Simply switch the titles!
And, so like the line in *My Fair Lady*.
> When Professor Higgins musically
> protests the mispronunciations of the
> English, he compares them to the French:
> "The French never care what they do,
> actually, as long as they pronounce
> it properly."
>> Ah! So with sin!

Let's have no fancy phrases for it! I am not an advocate
of that claptrap psychiatry that writes off evil as a
bad dream or a childish maladjustment.

> I resent the slick, newfangled faces that we
> put on evil.

We disguise it with a word like: "slip up."

> I read that the other day. A girl had
> run away from town, had lived with over
> forty men, and now was packed off to a
> home for unwed mothers. But, the
> social worker said:
>> "It was a slip up." So!

The more she practiced it, the less she knew about it.

> You cannot afford a casual experiment with that!

Take *Lust*. It currently enjoys the sanction of
          statistical encouragement.

          The Kinsey research has presented documented,
          scientific evidence of promiscuity. There isn't
          any question that it represents majority behavior.
          It's the average and normal thing to do, accord-
          ing to authenticated facts.

          What should I do, then, as a minister? Should I
          advise the youngsters in the church:

                    "Go to it! I can't argue facts!"

          Or should I strip the false façade from evil
          and proclaim:

                    "While chastity may be outnumbered,

                    it will never be outmoded! Keep to that!"

          There was another day of immorality recorded in
          the book called, *Only Yesterday,* a history
          of these United States throughout the "roaring
          twenties." Some of you recall those flaming days
          of flappers and the flask. The author tells about
          the number one best seller of the times, in which
          the heroine maintains no less than some 259 love
          affairs without showing "any real interest" in
          any one of them.

                    Well, that's to be expected!

          For, says Frederick Lewis Allen in his comment:

                    "The moment love becomes casual, it
                    becomes commonplace as well!"

Or *Greed:* that niggardly fuss-budgeting that pulls the
drawstrings.

>It does not amass tall fortunes
>but keeps short accounts.

Men make it "varra weel respectit" by the name of
"thrift," but it's a shriveling astringent that reduces
life.

>One often comes upon it in the church.
>How many post a sentinel upon the
>surplus, and anoint their officers custodians
>of the endowment.

They apply the yardstick of pinch-penny thrift, and
>when the ledgers cancel, Christ has come
>victorious away.
>When assets balance liabilities, the Lord
>is magnified indeed!
>When one and one make two, we enter in His
>courts with praise!
>It all goes by the names of caution,
>>common-sense,
>>>economy.

>But I do not believe in Fact, Father Almighty
>of the Universe;
>I don't believe in the Divinity of the Decimal
>Point;
>I don't believe in the Holy Catholic Calculus,
>or in the Resurrection of the Slide Rule.
>No! But, I believe in God,

Whose life was spendthrift and whose
vast extravagance has shamed my soul!
Or *Sloth,* the laziness of studied calm, continually
unperturbed, and apathetic to all possible appeals.

It is the *savoir-faire* that is forever heedless
of impending doom.

Hear Dr. Fosdick in his own confessional:
"The most powerful temptations in my
life have not been to do something
criminal and wrong, but to do nothing,
or to take a neutral shade when I ought
to stand out!"

Ah, Sloth!

Its gesture is the shrug,
Its motto is "so what?"
Its verdict is "thumbs down!"

It's the seduction of inertia,

the allurement of acquiescence, and
the enticement of nonchalance.

The former President of the United States, Dwight
Eisenhower, wrote about it in *Crusade in Europe.*

"Thoughtful Frenchmen frequently dis-
cussed with me the reasons for their
national collapse in 1940. I did not
find any Frenchmen who agreed that it was
the Maginot Line. They felt their diffi-
culties came about because of internal
weaknesses. 'We defeated ourselves

from within. We tried to oppose a four-
day work week against Germany's seven-
day week!' "

Or *Envy*, the *reductio ad absurdum* that diminishes
humanity down to the lowest common denominator.
Our homogenized society commends it to us as "together-
ness" and its activities are:

falling into step and hopping onto bandwagons.
Every numbskull nonentity insists on hauling
every hero down.
We simply cannot stand success. . . in other
people!
So, we ridicule the excellent, and
snub attainment.

I was angered and amazed to come upon a sentence
recently which said:

"Professors, eggheads, crackpots and subsersives."
They were lumped together. Well, it is an old
technique, familiar to this century. We cast
suspicion on the wise and honored. We enlarge
their eccentricities. We say:
"See there, you thought they were so
smart when they were just peculiar."

Envy's motto is:

Vox populi, vox Dei!" And it says:
"The people's voice is like the voice
of God!"

Don't you believe it for a moment, for the

equal level is the lowest level man can stand
upon: the flat mud-bottom of disastrous
mediocrity.

         Ah, Envy!

Its adherents called Christ "crazy," and, in
general,

> put roadblocks in the way of progress,
> and a veto on the voices of the prophets.
> They went nodding, "never, never," to
> each new idea.

The greatest leveler on earth has made the
nincompoop its standard.

(C. S. Lewis, in *The World's Last Night*,
composed its valedictory:

> "Here is someone who speaks English
> rather more clearly and euphoniously
> than I; it must be a vile, upstage,
> lah-di-dah affectation. Here's a
> fellow who says he doesn't like hot
> dogs . . . thinks himself too good
> for them, no doubt. Here's a man
> who hasn't turned on the jukebox . . .
> he's one of those goddam highbrows
> and is doing it to show off. If they
> were honest-to-God all right Joes,
> they'd be like me.
>
>   They've no business to be different!"

That sly deceiver, sin! These random samples must con-

vince you that if you should once attempt it, it will
play the part of virtue.

It will decorate itself for good behavior, and
orate its own superiority, but then, beware!

The more you practice it, the less you know about it! So,
The more that you avoid it, the better you can meet it.

No, I do not advocate the nunnery and hermitage. Sin does
exist. Christ on a Cross was not a Kodachrome projected
on a cloud bank!

But, avoid it while you can!

The name of Oscar Wilde has been synonymous
with human frailty. His life was overrun
with hungry things that gnawed at him.

His life was wasted, and the final verdict on his
days was written by a wiser man who said:

"He had success without dignity,
and failure without pathos."

Well, how did he come to that? He ran to
vice as others run for home. One time he
tossed the flippant line:

"The only way to be rid of temptation is to yield to it."

So, one conquers by compliance! It's so
cowardly to turn from evil!

"Aren't you man enough to try yourself against it? Let's give in
a little!"

> Famous last words of the
> lost souls of the world!

Who is the person best equipped to come to
grips with sin?
You tell me, who?
Some sodden derelict who knows it intimately,
every turn and twist; now can he say,

> "Leave everything to me; I'll get
> you out of it!"

You tell me, who?
The rock-ribbed sensible protagonist who has
refused it stubbornly time and again:
cannot he say:

> "Here is my hand, and by God, you
> shall not go down!"

The more that you avoid it, then, the better
you can meet it.

Recently, I was a speaker on a college campus, and was
afterward invited to a dormitory session. I was snapped
up to attention when a student asked:

> "Since you're a minister, you probably
> don't know; but, anyhow, why shouldn't
> anybody be promiscuous, since every-
> body is?"

I told her that we clergymen are not so isolated
as she thinks. We do see sin. We see it at
the sleazy end of its innocuous beginning, when
the mask is off . . . and when the blotched,

corroded face of slobbering lust sits down and
sobs at what it has committed . . . ah, we see
it, when it is too late! Few people recognize
it when it first arrives. Nobody ever says
to me:

"Say, Reverend, I'm thinking, more
or less, of taking out another fellow's wife:
all right with you?"

No one says that. But, when his infidelity
has been discovered, when it all spills out,
and when the moral ambulance comes screaming
for the soul, and when all hell breaks loose,
then everybody sees it . . . at the end!

Sin is a dangerous foe, and a deadly enemy.

God doesn't lead us into it, but only He can help us
out of it.

The best thing we can do is pray:

"Our Father, don't let us experiment
with evil!"

VIII

THINE THE GLORY

Thine Is the Glory Forever and Ever!

Glorifying God has always been the recreation of His saints.
  Their lives were kindled into fervor,
      provoked into eloquence,
          and excited into gallantry!
    There was a fanfare to their faith,
          and their belief was punctuated by an
          exclamation point!
But, the majority of worshipers approach the Lord as
though they had been taken into custody and booked
for nonsupport!
      They have a hangdog look,
          a hesitating step,
              and humdrum interest.
For them, religion is a grumbling prohibition, not a
glorious prerogative.
          What Dr. Halford Luccock calls a "spiritual
          arthritis" has set in and crippled their responses.
          Nowhere in the world are people more perverse
          than in the presence of their Lord.

>They stand stiff-legged at the altar,
>and their posture is defiant in the
>face of deity.

They won't relinquish their self-adulation
for the sake of anybody, no, not even God!
The German poet, Rainer Maria Rilke, once
paraded in his
arrogance before the altar when he wrote:

>"What will you do, God, when I die,
>When I, your pitcher, shattered lie?"

And in America, the homegrown species is as
insolent.

I am amused by Clarence Day's remembrance of
his family entitled *Life With Father*. But I don't
appreciate the humor of his father's attitude
toward God. He tells us that:

>"Father expected a good deal of God.
>He didn't actually accuse God of gross
>inefficiency, but when he prayed, his
>tone was loud and angry, like that
>of a dissatisfied guest in a care-
>lessly-managed hotel!"

>Perverse and peevish!

When the matins sound, you know whose name
will get the glory;
when the vespers chime, cannot you guess before
whose image every knee will bow?

>His name is man!

His symbol is the mirror;
His cathedral is the commonplace;
And his *Te Deum Laudamus* is dedicated
to himself.

He needs to be chastised by the formidable remembrance
of his catechism. It begins its cold instruction with
the question:

"What is man's chief end?" And then astonishes
the student with a rollicking reply:

"To glorify God and to enjoy Him forever!"
So! "God hath exalted Him and given Him the name above
all other names, that at the name of Jesus every knee
should bow unto the Glory of the Father!"

"Thine the Glory!"

If you should define that for behavior, it
suggests that glorifying God means, first of
all, to

Credit Him. "To give the credit where the credit's due."
If there is something elemental in the sound of this;
if you suspect me of a kindergarten pedagogy, leading
you by tiny hands into the obvious, it is because this
has escaped us in our sophistry.

What man controls the universe?

Can you, by fingertip control,
ignite the sky?
Who lights the starwicks at the
turn of dusk?
Who strings the sheets of snow upon

the washline of the night?
Who ladles out the sun at dawn?
Who fluffs the blossoms out upon
the bough?
Who rolls the thunderheads along the
valley of the winds?
> Who does these things?
> The infant, man?
And when he wanders weary home, then
does he pull the night around his
shoulders and put out the stars?
Let him remember Maltbie Babcock's
genealogy:
"Back of the loaf is the snowy flour,
And back of the flour the mill.
and back of the mill is the wheat and
the shower,
> And the sun and the Father's will."

Instead of glorifying God, most men defame Him!
If you want to do it, you can make a case against the Lord.
It is the simplest task in all the world.

We all feel set upon by fate, and think we are
the most misused of creatures. Let the acids
of self-pity trickle through your days, and
you can turn the litmus paper pink with strong
resentments!
Dorothy Parker, that sardonic wit, has made a
capsule of her cynicism:

> "Oh, hard is the struggle and sparse is
> The gain of the one at the top,
> For art is a form of catharsis
> And love is a permanent flop,
> And work is the province of cattle
> And rest's for a clam in a shell,
> So I'm thinking of chucking the battle;
> Would you kindly direct me to Hell?"

Or H. L. Mencken was another carp who never changed his tune. He wrote to Will Durant in 1933:

> "The act of worship, as carried on by
> Christians, seems to me to be debasing
> rather than ennobling! It involves
> groveling before a Being who, if He
> really exists, deserves to be denounced
> rather than respected. On the con-
> trary, it seems to me that on the
> strength of His daily acts, He must
> be set down as a most stupid, cruel, and
> villainous fellow!"

So, if we compose a laundry list of dirty linen, and recite a ritual of mean complaints, no wonder that the wonder is gone out of us!

> Of course, a man can make a case against
> the Lord! But if he does, he isn't
> telling us a thing about Divinity, he's
> telling us a lot about himself.

Real praise can hunch above a sick bed and recite: "Praise
ye the Lord."
Real praise can stand in black beside the grave and say:
"Blessed be God!"
Real praise can slump beneath a failure and still sing
doxologies!

The classical case history of suffering is Job in the
Old Testament.
He is the broken symbol of unbroken faith. He had lost
everything. He was encamped beneath the foothills of
misfortune, and its shadow fell across him. Life was dark.
When his tormentors found him, he was muttering alone:

> "The Lord has given, and the
> Lord has taken."

> And they smiled a knowing smile; it was a
> sentence of defeat. But, in the same breath,
> Job continued:

> "Blessed be the name of God!"

But even when the cornucopia is full, so many men are
niggardly in adoration.

> They are "neon" Christians, and the instant
> that you pull the plug, then their religion stops.
> A member of another church I served once raged
> at me for turning toward the Cross by way of ges-
> ture.
> He refused to kneel when he was made an Elder,
> for he thought that all of this was "ostentatious"

in the house of God. You may imagine my surprise when I encountered this "defender of the
faith," who wanted his religion plain, arrayed in
plumage fit for peacocks at the meeting of his
lodge. What he denied the King of Kings,
          he gave unstintingly to hocus-pocus!
So, instead of glorifying God, so many use the faith to
glorify themselves. Instead of losing life to find it,
they display themselves to the applauding populace.
          Who cares whose name is at the top,
                whose motion saved the day
                      whose solo starred the service? Ah,
                      "What matter, I or they,
                      Mine or another's day,
                      So the right word be said,
                      And life the sweeter made."
          Who cares? I ask you.
          What did Jesus care about the march of time, or
          avalanche of progress?
          Do you think He notices the mark you make upon
society, or that He flutters with excitement at
          your notoriety?
          Do you think He sits above the conference room
          and notes the long debates?
Absurd! You will give glory if you give the credit where
          the credit's due!
                And we must!

Celebrate the Lord!

There's nothing ornamental in the music of our souls:
>   No bright cadenzas,
>
>   no embroidered obbligatos,
>
>   and no spangled descants!

What I am saying is: The most neglected song of faith today is PRAISE!

>   One seldom hears a "Holy, Holy, Holy!" in the house of God.
>
>   We stamp the flashfires of amazement,
>
>   We adulterate the wine of wonder, and
>
>   we snip the feathers of the
>
>   skylark on the wing!

I tell you that the church of Jesus Christ ran through the ancient pagan world upon a single cylinder. Says Dr. Luccock:

>   "Christianity made its way throughout the Roman world by the communication of wonder!"
>
>   I believe it did. For, men had had enough of household deities, and gods of small utility.
>
>   This new faith caught hold of their farthest-flung imagination, for He took His time by such surprise that it could only sputter, as it staggered back from Him:
>
>   "Why, we have seen strange things today!"
>
>   He scandalized society!
>
>   He ruffled every tradition that they knew!
>
>   See! God on earth: an intimate divinity.

Death on a Cross: a loving Saviour! And
an open tomb: eternal life!
They stood enchanted, and at last when breath
broke through, they sang, *Gloria in Excelsis!*
Praise, of course, becomes the measurement of
faith, not deeds.
Good deeds are often done by charlatans and
fakers.
Aye, most men behave because they have to, and
they don't get any credit on the ledger sheet
for that!
But no one counterfeits a genuine enthusiasm.
If you love your God, for God's sake,
tell Him so!
I think that He revealed more of Himself through ques-
tions than through answers, and it seems to me that He was
most concerned to know:
"Whom say ye that I am?" What did men
think of Him?
When they engaged in admiration and in adula-
tion, He was pleased. The Lord was happiest
when Peter cried; "Thou art the Christ!"
When someone said: "Lord, I believe!"
And when the multitudes called their
hosannas on His head, and
the disciples thought it smacked of osten-
tation, Jesus said:

"Don't stop them! For if they were silent,
then the very stones would call my name!"
Now to be honest, Jesus is a jealous God who loves to be
festooned with Glory. There is something to be said for
ceremony in the church. You do not glorify your God by
stark utilitarianism and by antiseptic architecture.

There's a frill to faith! It thrives
best on extravagance!

I can't forget an installation sermon preached by
Dr. Joseph Sizoo. It was twined about an obscure
text whose words were these:

"Upon the top of the pillar, there
was lily-work!"

And I remember what he made of it. Said he:
"Nobody saw the high parts of the pillars.
They were decorated for the sight of God
alone. It was an act of praise!"
God likes it when we gild the lily and
shellac the stars! And,
I can tell you that He wants to be made
much of!

Listen to this verse.

It is the last verse of the Gospel of Luke. Jesus
Christ has gone and left the world a lonely and a
wretched place. An inventory of His time would
list a host of implacable foes,
inevitable hostilities, and
unavoidable defeats.

You'd think that the disciples would be getting
shoulders to the wheel,
> hands to the plow, and
>> noses to the grindstone.

Life was running out on them; they only had a
wisp of time in which to take their century! But
listen to this text. How did they go about this
business?

> "They were," said Luke, "continually in the
> temple, praising God!"

> A waste of time? Ah, no!

> That gave them their incentives; how that
> tuned their lives into a great chorale!

Now, if you really love your God, for God's sake, tell Him
so!

> Now, what did Mary say of Him: "My soul doth
> magnify the Lord!"

> And Paul, how did he speak of faith: "Rejoice,
> again I say, rejoice!"

> How did St. Francis look upon the Lord? His word
> was: "Alleluia!"

Now, I say to you, the church is lighted by these chande-
liers of praise, these clustered glorias and bright doxologies! I say to you go, strip the Bible of its "Glory Be's" and
"Praise the Lords" and what is left will not be worth
the keeping!

So! Let us be honest in the face of God.

We have a history of niggardly neglect. Right at the first, men welshed upon their adoration.

Up there, riding out the darkness, Jesus saw the way the world was going.

Aye, let me remind you that He paid!

You cost something!

In these days of pinnacled prices, let me say that the most overrated and inflated article on earth is you, yourself!

Christ on a Cross! He paid, and He who gave a God's ransom for a beggar's brood,

has seldom heard His Name in praise!

Some time ago, that mastercraftsman of the English tongue, Sir Winston Churchill, salted down a speech with sailor talk. He told of how a gob once saved a drowning boy. The sailor heard the screeches of the lad, leaped into Plymouth harbour at the risk of life, and lugged him safe to shore. When it was over, then the mother came to him and asked:

"Are you the man who saved my little boy?" Expecting some reward, the sailor boasted that he was.

"Well, then!" she huffed, "where is his cap?"

Indeed, it sickens me to see the bunting hung for some small patriotic

jag, or else to hear the shouts for some inconsequential idol!
      Where, then, are the ranks of faith?
      Who strikes its colors, and who shakes the heavens
      with the wild reverberations of His name?
      Go, let the trumpets take the tune and teach it to
      the skies!
      "Heaven and earth are full of Thy Glory,
      Glory be to Thee, O Lord!"

ACKNOWLEDGMENTS

I   THE PERFECT PARADOX

1. Day Lewis, C. From "The Magnetic Mountain" in *Collected Poems*. Copyright 1935 by C. Day Lewis. Used with permission of Harold Matson Company.
2. Gurney, Dorothy Frances Blomfield. "The Lord God Planted a Garden." London: Burns and Oates, Ltd., 1933.
3. Shaw, Bernard. *St. Joan*. London: The Society of Authors, 1923.

II   THE UNCOMMON DENOMINATOR

1. Trueblood, Dr. Elton. *Foundations for Reconstruction*. New York: Harper & Brothers, 1946.
2. Studdert-Kennedy, G. A. "Indifference" from *The Sorrows of God*. New York: Harper & Brothers. Used by permission.
3. Sayers, Dorothy. *Creed or Chaos?* New York: Harcourt, Brace & World, Inc., 1949.
4. Galsworthy, John. *The Mob*. New York: Charles Scribner's Sons, 1914.
5. Auden, W. H. *For the Time Being*. Copyright 1944, W. H. Auden. Reprinted from *The Collected Poetry of W. H. Auden*. By permission of Random House, Inc., New York.

III   LIVING LIFE INSIDE OUT

1. Huxley, Aldous. *Ape and Essence*. New York: Harper & Brothers, 1948.

IV   UNDER NEW MANAGEMENT

1. Sherwood, Robert. *Abe Lincoln in Illinois.* New York: Charles Scribner's Sons, 1939.
2. Fosdick, Harry Emerson. *What Is Vital in Religion.* New York: Harper and Brothers, 1955.

V   ALL OR NOTHING AT ALL

1. Fosdick, Harry Emerson, (*op. cit.*)

VI   THE QUALITY OF MERCY

1. Shaw, Bernard. *Major Barbara.* London: The Society of Authors, 1905.
2. Auden, W. H., (*op. cit.*)
3. Shaw, Bernard. *St. Joan.* London: The Society of Authors, 1923.
4. Lewis, C. S. From *Christian Behavior* in *Mere Christianity.* Copyright © 1952 by The Macmillan Company. Used by permission.

VII   TINKERING WITH TRAGEDY

1. Lewis, C. S., (*op cit.*)
2. Lerner, Alan Jay, and Loewe, Frederick. *My Fair Lady.* Copyright © 1956 by Alan Jay Lerner and Frederick Loewe. Chappell & Co. Inc., New York, N.Y., Publisher and Owner of allied rights throughout the world.
3. Allen, Frederick Lewis. *Only Yesterday.* New York: Harper & Brothers, 1957.
4. Fosdick, Harry Emerson. *The Power to See It Through.* New York: Harper & Brothers, 1935.

5. Eisenhower, Dwight D. *Crusade in Europe*. New York: Doubleday & Company, Inc., 1948. Used by permission.
6. Lewis, C. S. *The World's Last Night*. New York: Harcourt, Brace & World, Inc., 1960.

VIII   THINE THE GLORY

1. Day, Clarence. *God and My Father*. New York: Alfred A. Knopf, Inc., 1932.
2. Babcock, Maltbie. "Give Us This Day Our Daily Bread."
3. Parker, Dorothy. "Coda" from *Sunset Gun*. New York: The Viking Press, Inc., 1928.
4. Durant, Will. *On the Meaning of Life*. Ray Long and Richard Smith, 1932.
5. Luccock, Halford E. *Communicating the Gospel*. New York: Harper & Brothers, 1954.